FINGERPICKING
FILM SCORE MUSIC

CONTENTS

INTRODUCTION TO FINGERSTYLE GUITAR

Fingerstyle (a.k.a. fingerpicking) is a guitar technique that means you literally pick the strings with your right-hand fingers and thumb. This contrasts with the conventional technique of strumming and playing single notes with a pick (a.k.a. flatpicking). For fingerpicking, you can use any type of guitar: acoustic steel-string, nylon-string classical, or electric.

THE RIGHT HAND

The most common right-hand position is shown here.

Use a high wrist; arch your palm as if you were holding a ping-pong ball. Keep the thumb outside and away from the fingers, and let the fingers do the work rather than lifting your whole hand.

The thumb generally plucks the bottom strings with downstrokes on the left side of the thumb and thumbnail. The other fingers pluck the higher strings using upstrokes with the fleshy tip of the fingers and fingernails. The thumb and fingers should pluck one string per stroke and not brush over several strings.

Another picking option you may choose to use is called hybrid picking (a.k.a. plectrum-style fingerpicking). Here, the pick is usually held between the thumb and first finger, and the three remaining fingers are assigned to pluck the higher strings.

THE LEFT HAND

The left-hand fingers are numbered 1 through 4.

Be sure to keep your fingers arched, with each joint bent; if they flatten out across the strings, they will deaden the sound when you fingerpick. As a general rule, let the strings ring as long as possible when playing fingerstyle.

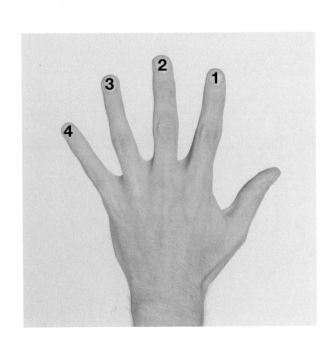

Braveheart - Main Title

from the Motion Picture BRAVEHEART

Music by James Horner

Drop D tuning:
(low to high) D-A-D-G-B-E

Chariots of Fire

from CHARIOTS OF FIRE

By Vangelis

Drop D tuning:
(low to high) D-A-D-G-B-E

Intro

Moderately

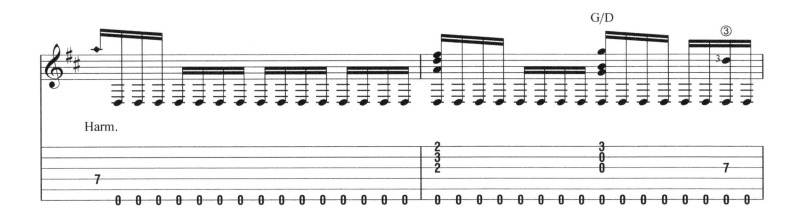

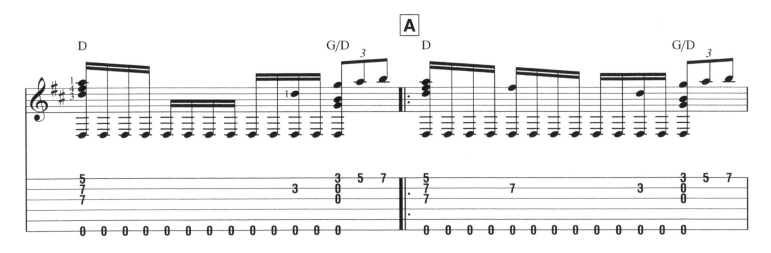

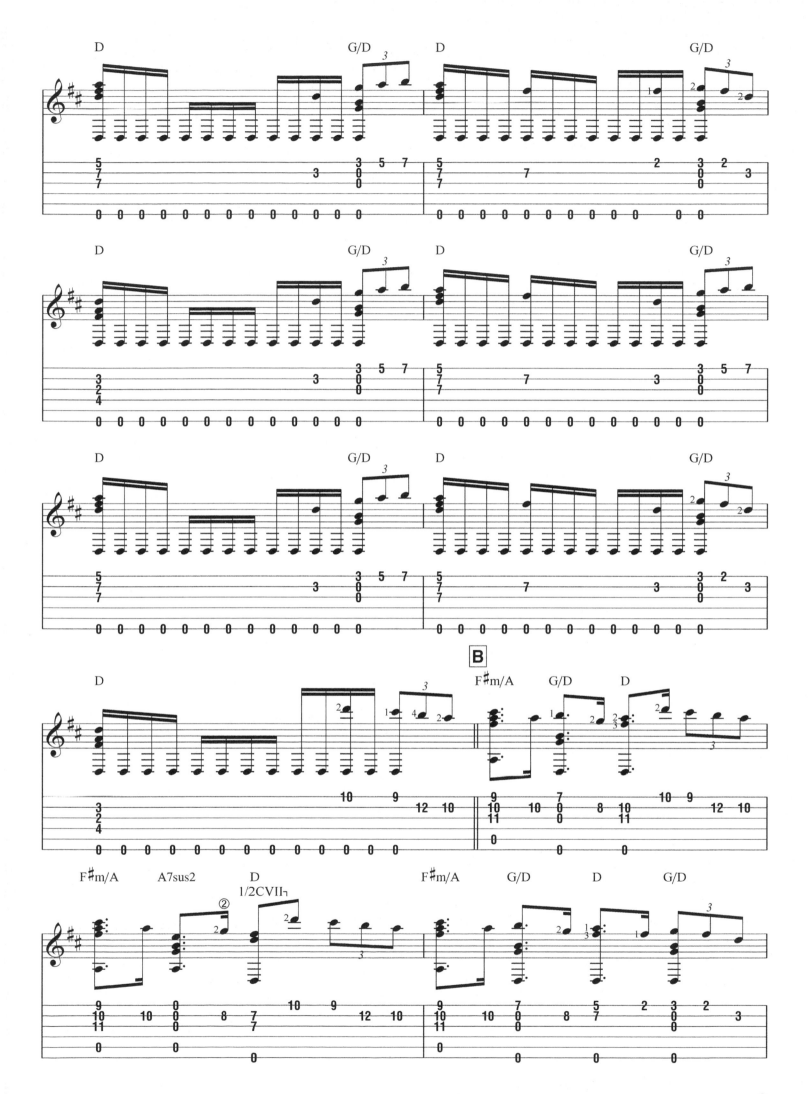

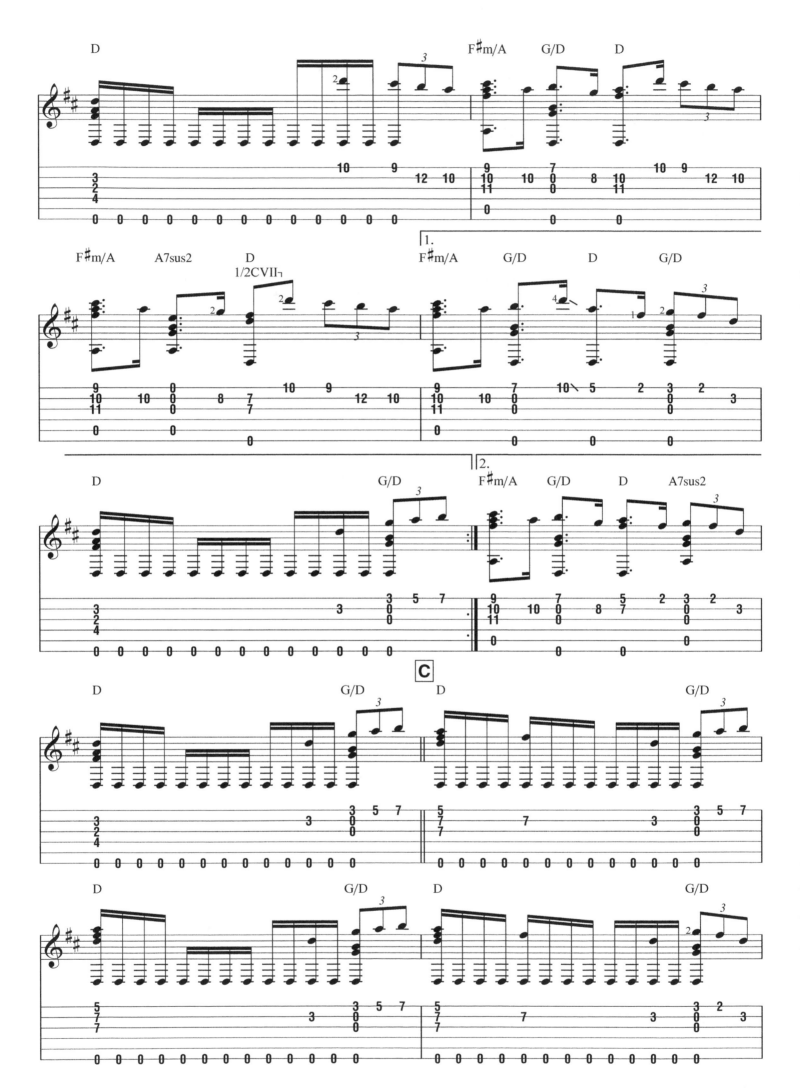

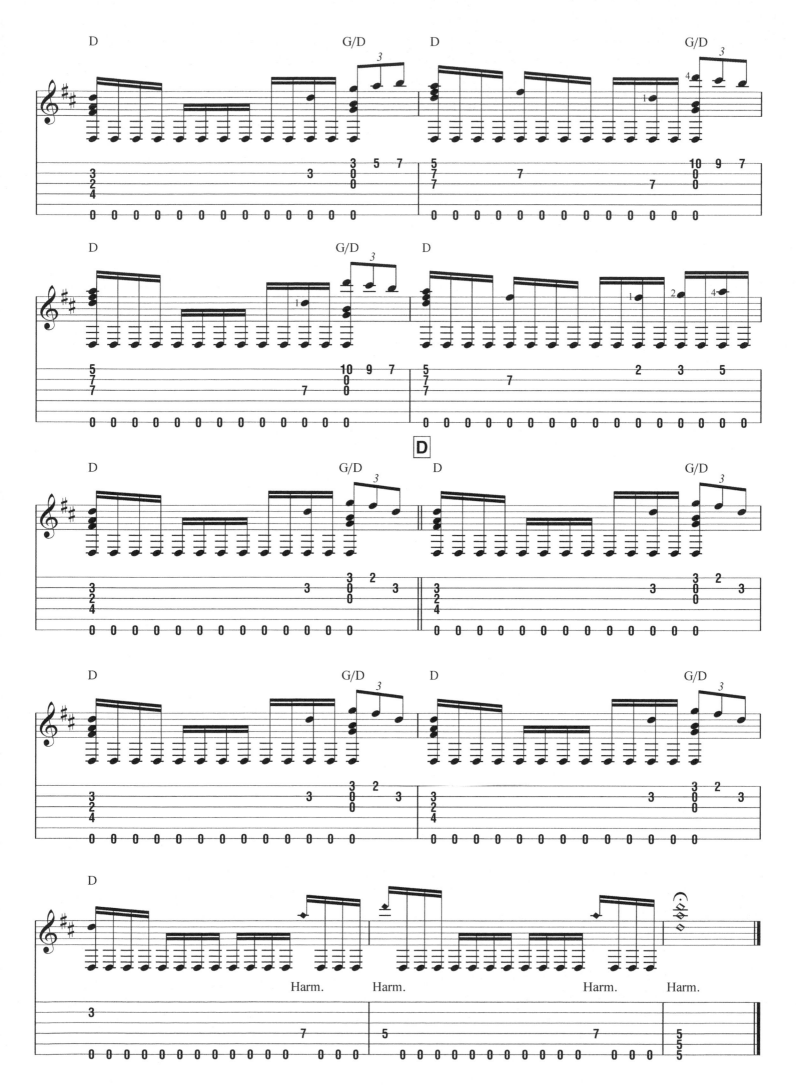

Gabriel's Oboe

from the Motion Picture THE MISSION

Music by Ennio Morricone

Drop D tuning:
(low to high) D-A-D-G-B-E

Moderately slow

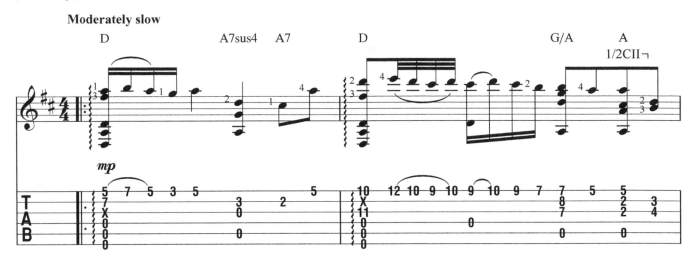

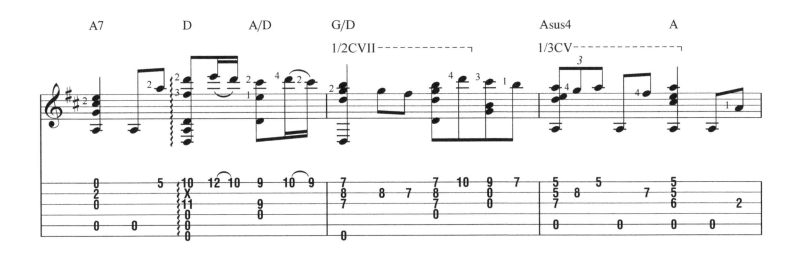

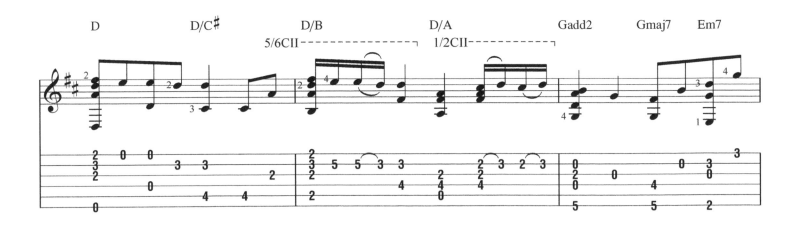

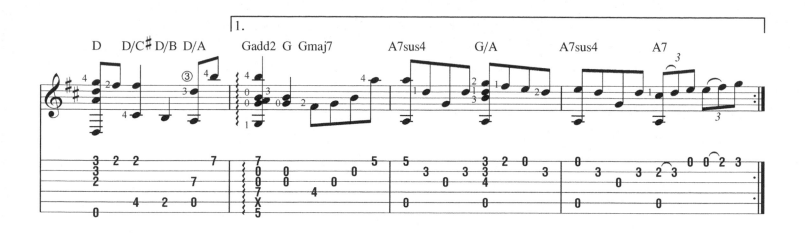

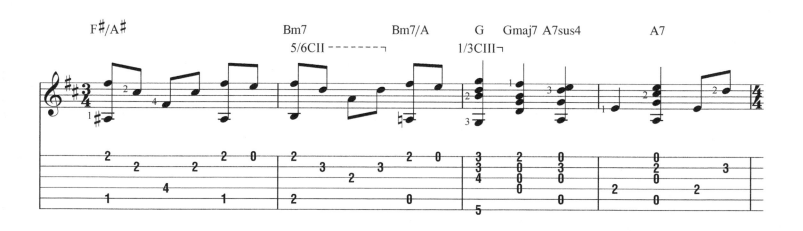

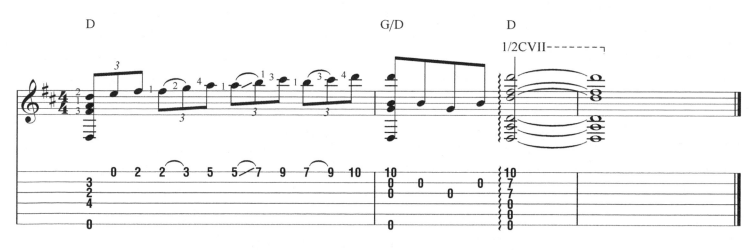

Hedwig's Theme

from the Motion Picture HARRY POTTER AND THE SORCERER'S STONE

Music by John Williams

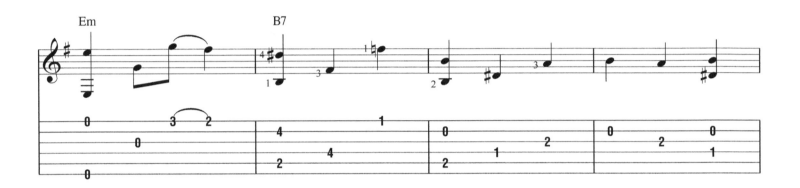

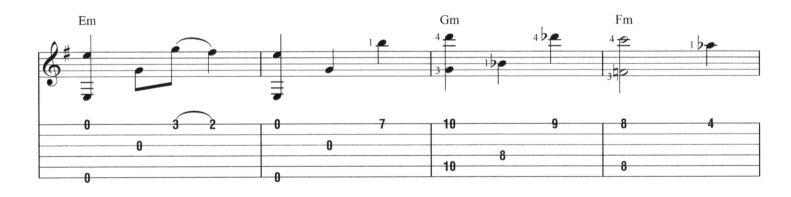

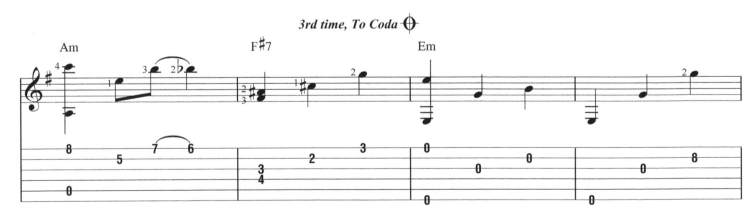

He's a Pirate

from PIRATES OF THE CARIBBEAN: THE CURSE OF THE BLACK PEARL

Music by Klaus Badelt, Geoffrey Zanelli and Hans Zimmer

Drop D tuning:
(low to high) D-A-D-G-B-E

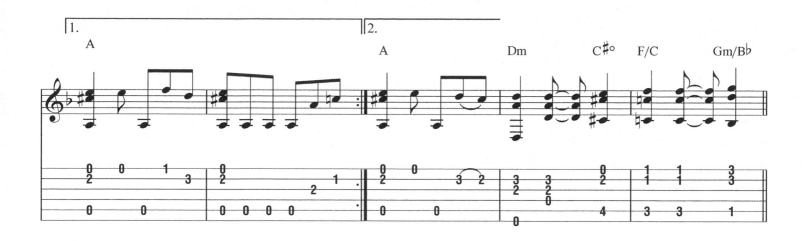

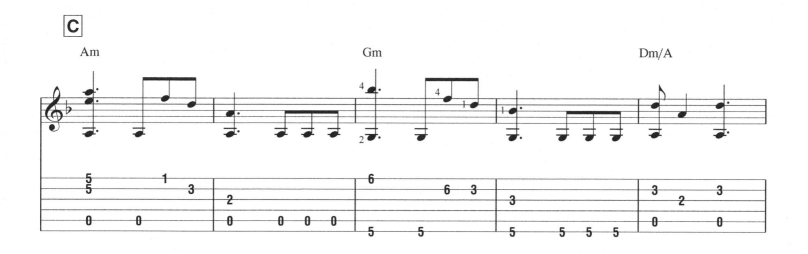

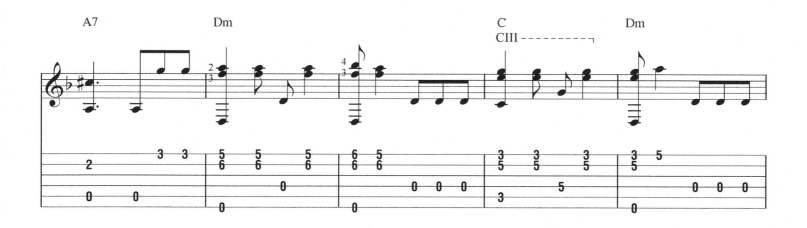

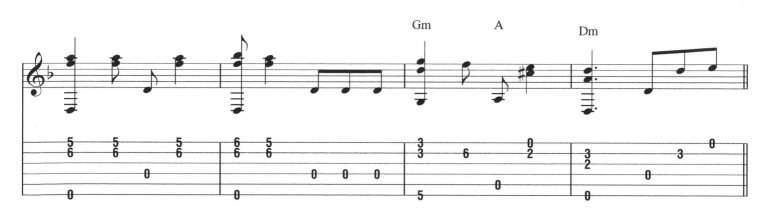

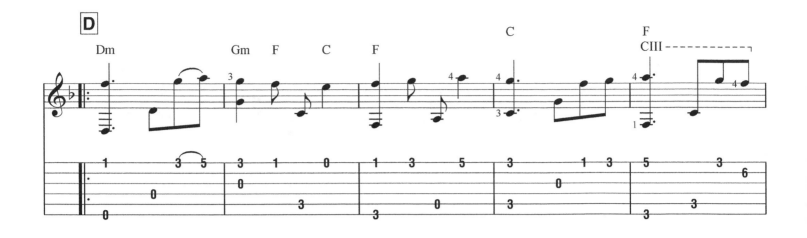

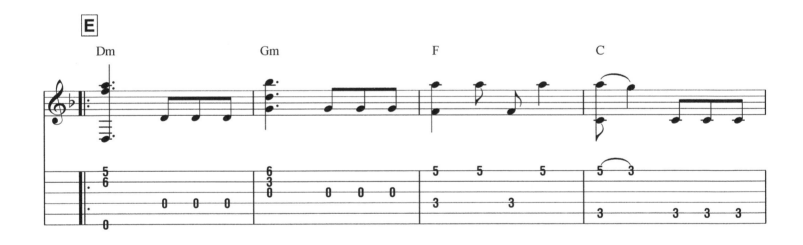

James Bond Theme

By Monty Norman

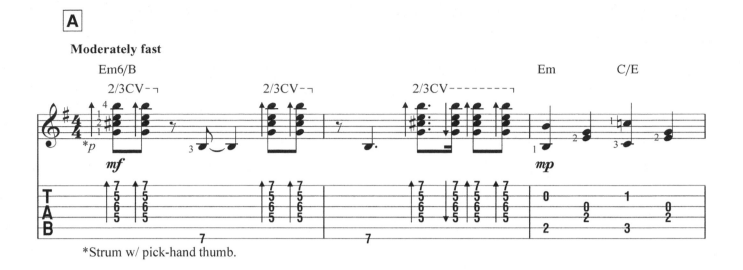

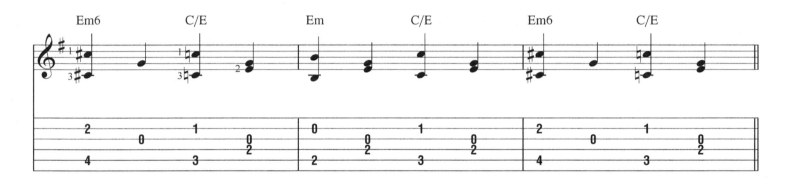

*Strum w/ pick-hand thumb.

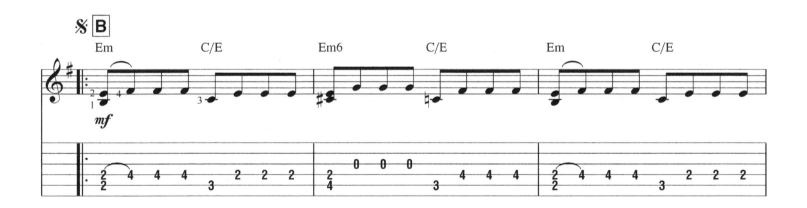

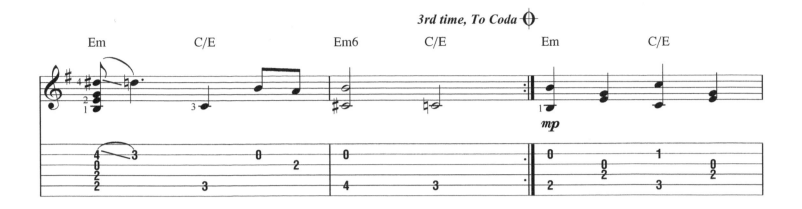

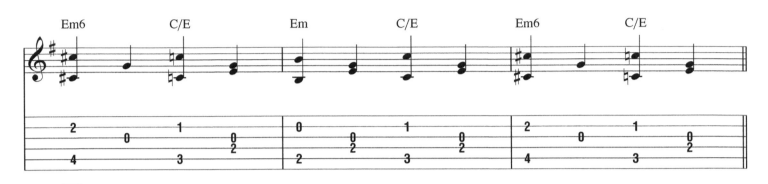

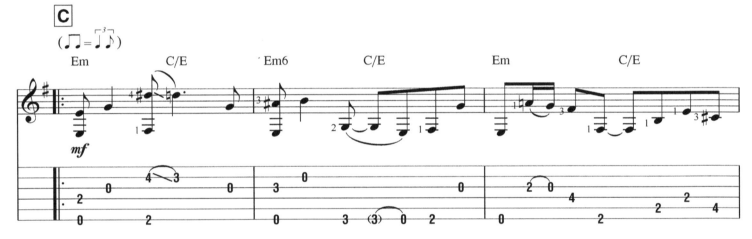

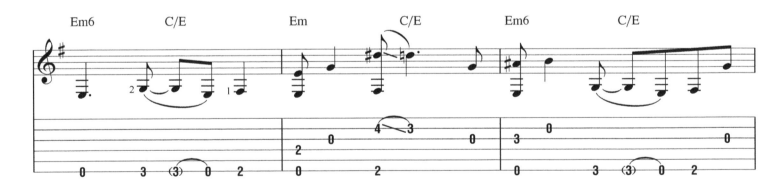

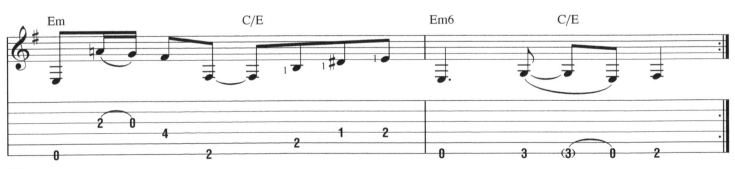

Last of the Mohicans
(Main Theme)

from the Twentieth Century Fox Motion Picture THE LAST OF THE MOHICANS

By Trevor Jones

Drop D tuning:
(low to high) D-A-D-G-B-E

Moderately slow

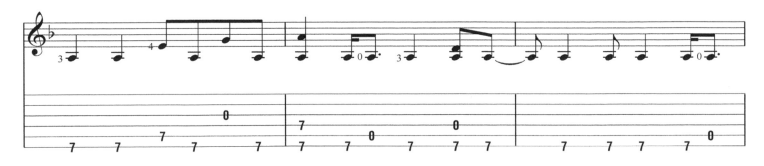

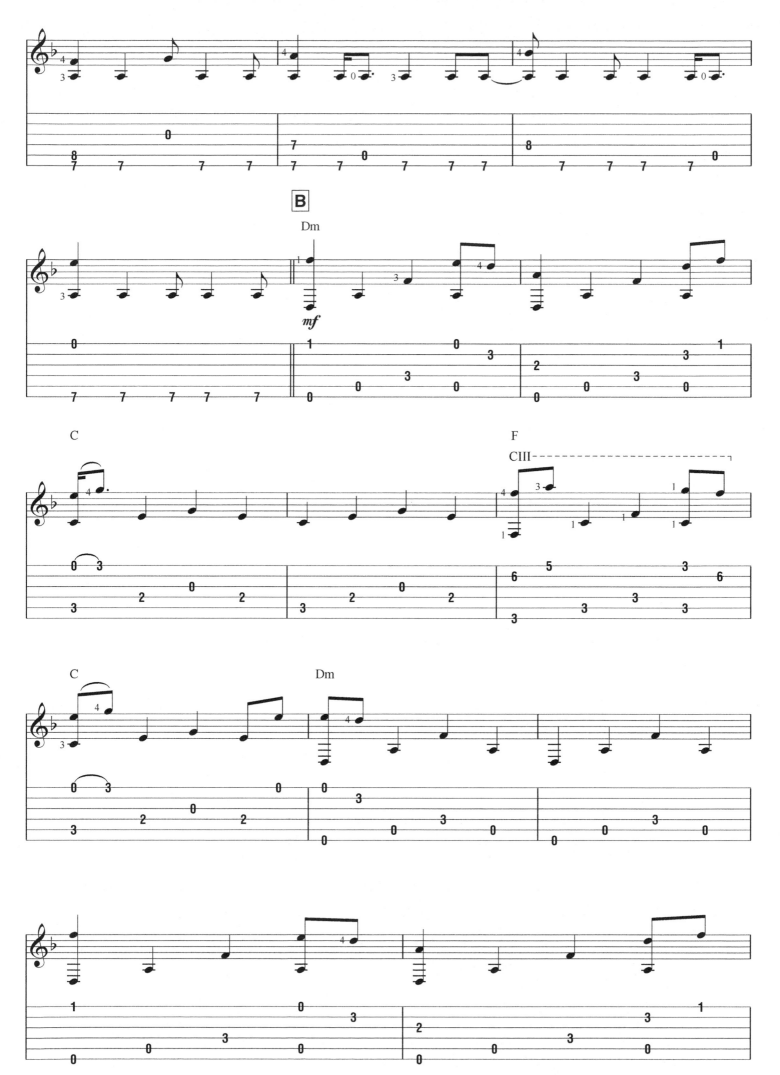

Legends of the Fall

from TriStar Pictures' LEGENDS OF THE FALL

Composed by James Horner

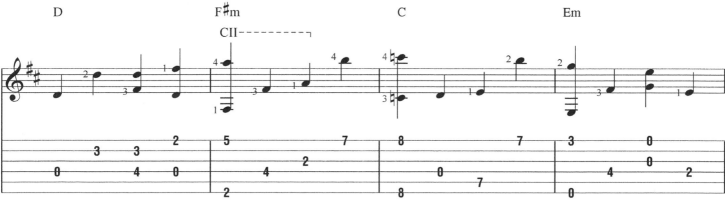

Theme from "Lawrence of Arabia"

from LAWRENCE OF ARABIA

By Maurice Jarre

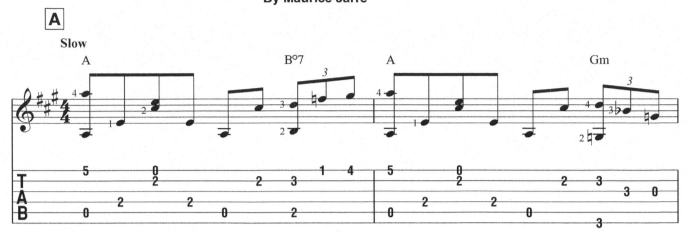

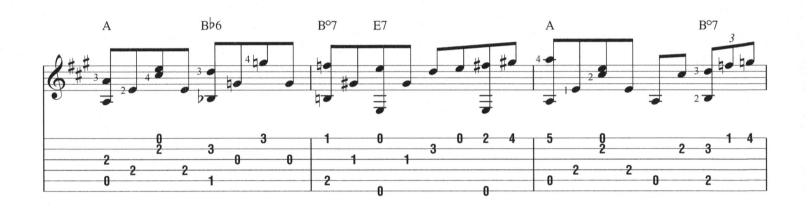

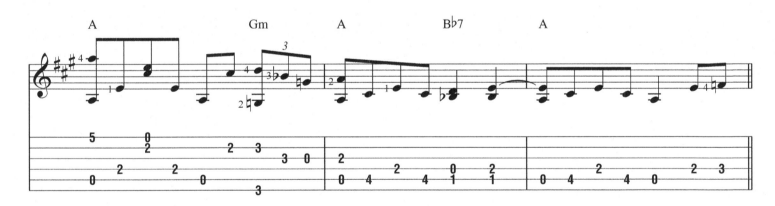

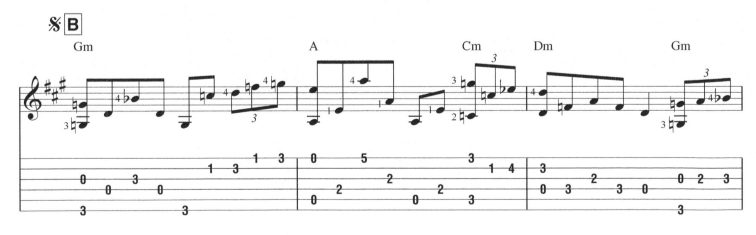

The Pink Panther

from THE PINK PANTHER

By Henry Mancini

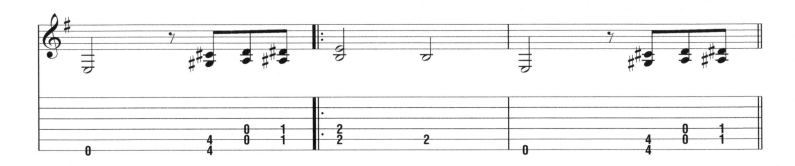

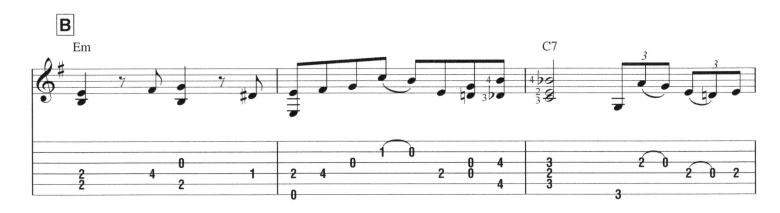

Raiders March

from the Paramount Motion Picture RAIDERS OF THE LOST ARK
Music by John Williams

Spartacus - Love Theme

from the Universal-International Picture Release SPARTACUS

By Alex North

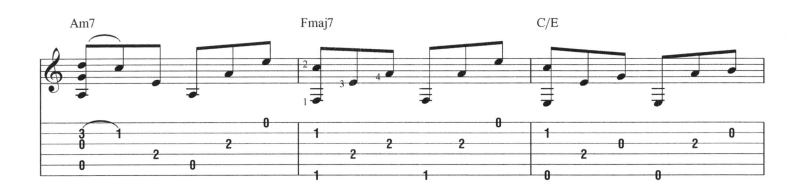

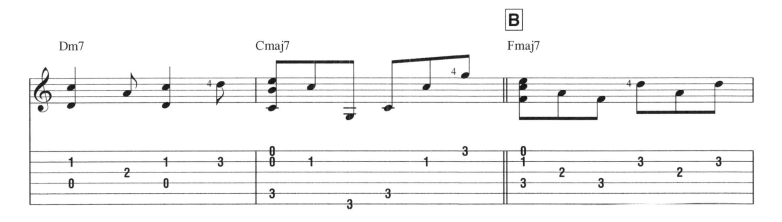

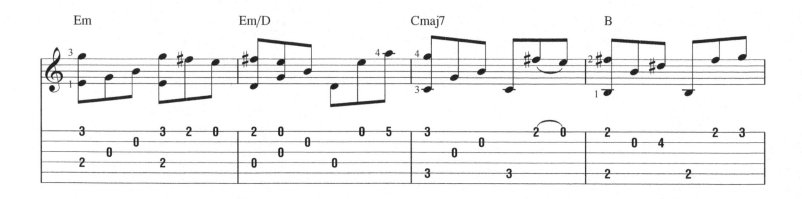

C

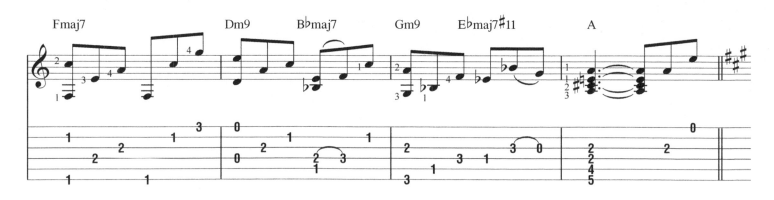

Theme from "Schindler's List"

from the Universal Motion Picture SCHINDLER'S LIST

Music by John Williams

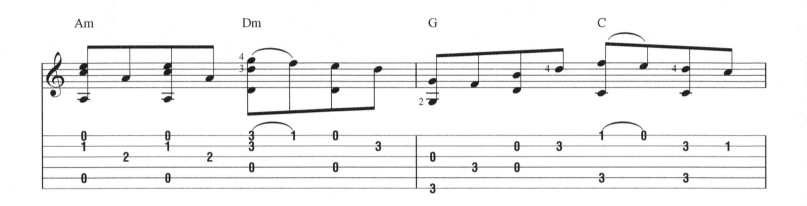

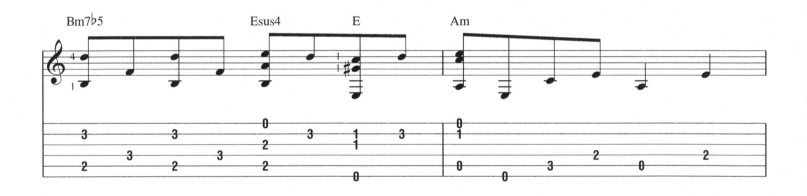

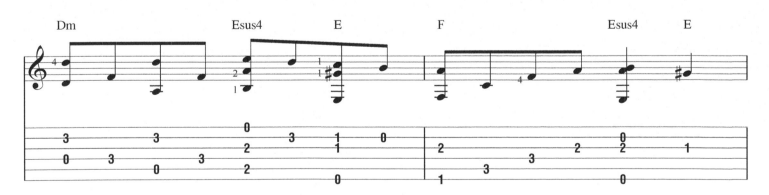

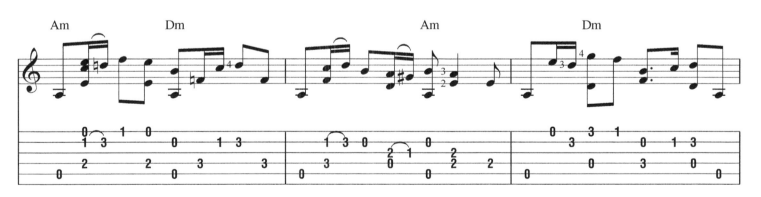

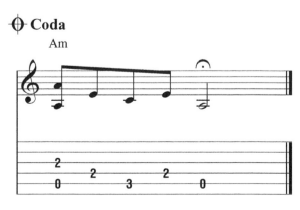

Star Wars (Main Theme)

from STAR WARS

Music by John Williams

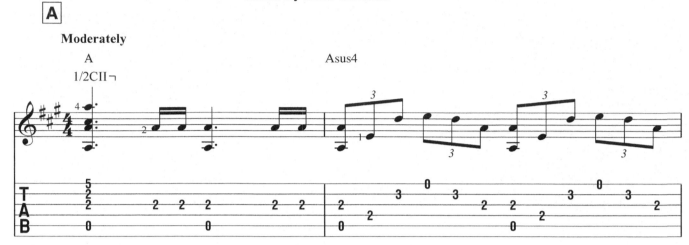

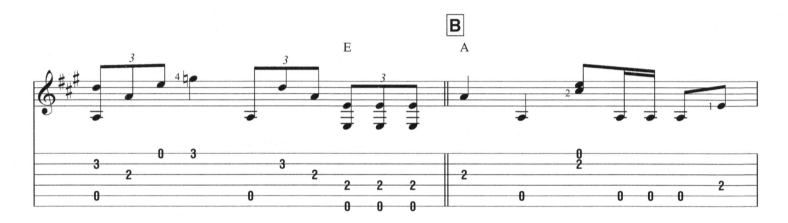

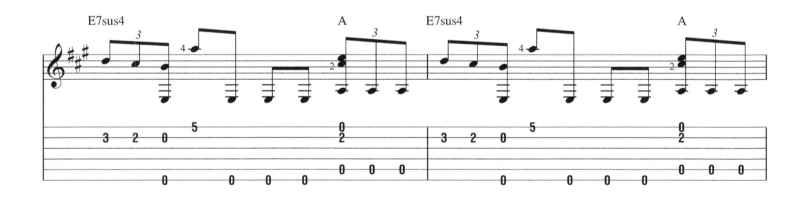

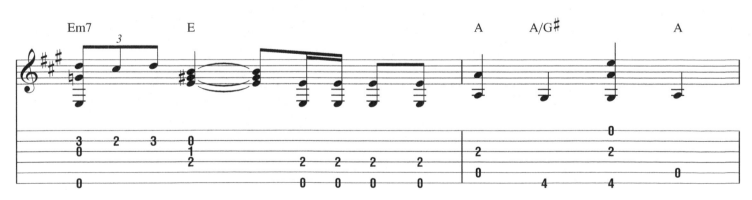

Theme from "Terms of Endearment"

from the Paramount Picture TERMS OF ENDEARMENT

By Michael Gore

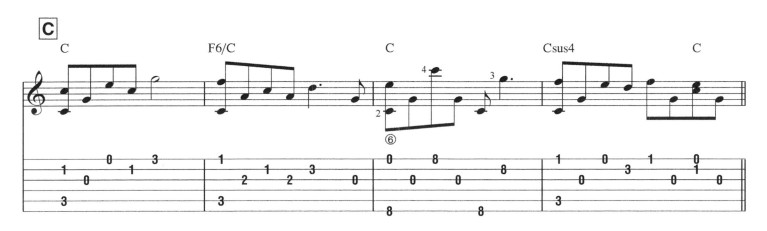

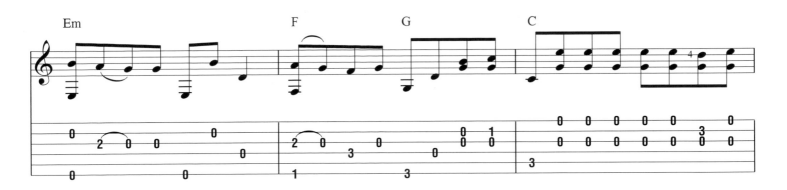

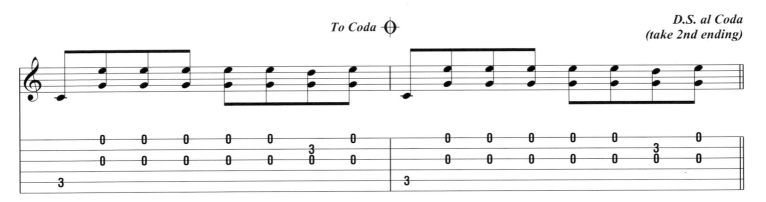

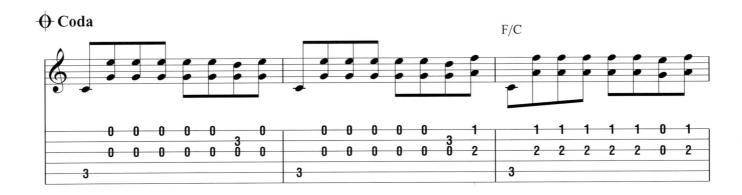

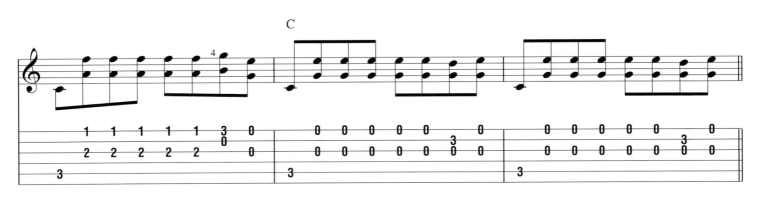

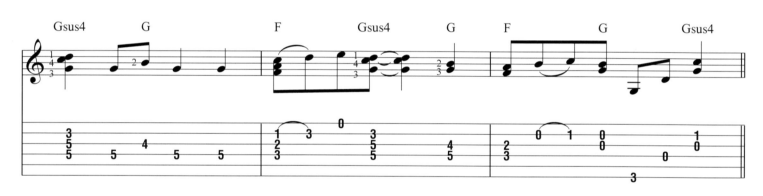

G

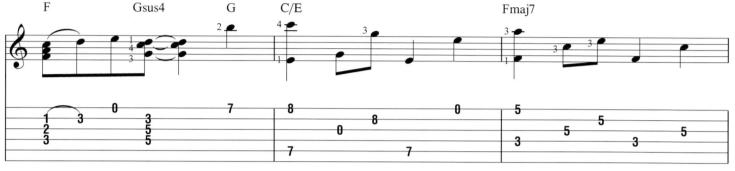

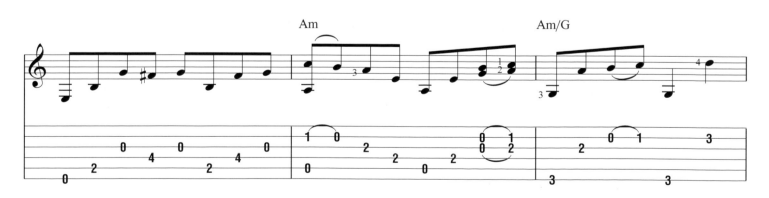

FINGERPICKING GUITAR BOOKS

Hone your fingerpicking skills with these great songbooks featuring solo guitar arrangements in standard notation and tablature. The arrangements in these books are carefully written for intermediate-level guitarists. Each song combines melody and harmony in one superb guitar fingerpicking arrangement. Each book also includes an introduction to basic fingerstyle guitar.

Fingerpicking Acoustic
00699614 15 songs.......................$14.99

Fingerpicking Acoustic Classics
00160211 15 songs.......................$16.99

Fingerpicking Acoustic Hits
00160202 15 songs.......................$12.99

Fingerpicking Acoustic Rock
00699764 14 songs.......................$16.99

Fingerpicking Ballads
00699717 15 songs.......................$14.99

Fingerpicking Beatles
00699049 30 songs.......................$24.99

Fingerpicking Beethoven
00702390 15 pieces.....................$10.99

Fingerpicking Blues
00701277 15 songs $10.99

Fingerpicking Broadway Favorites
00699843 15 songs.......................$9.99

Fingerpicking Broadway Hits
00699838 15 songs.......................$7.99

Fingerpicking Campfire
00275964 15 songs.......................$12.99

Fingerpicking Celtic Folk
00701148 15 songs.......................$12.99

Fingerpicking Children's Songs
00699712 15 songs.......................$9.99

Fingerpicking Christian
00701076 15 songs.......................$12.99

Fingerpicking Christmas
00699599 20 carols.....................$10.99

Fingerpicking Christmas Classics
00701695 15 songs.......................$7.99

Fingerpicking Christmas Songs
00171333 15 songs.......................$10.99

Fingerpicking Classical
00699620 15 pieces.....................$10.99

Fingerpicking Country
00699687 17 songs.......................$12.99

Fingerpicking Disney
00699711 15 songs.......................$16.99

Fingerpicking Early Jazz Standards
00276565 15 songs $12.99

Fingerpicking Duke Ellington
00699845 15 songs.......................$9.99

Fingerpicking Enya
00701161 15 songs.......................$16.99

Fingerpicking Film Score Music
00160143 15 songs.......................$12.99

Fingerpicking Gospel
00701059 15 songs.......................$9.99

Fingerpicking Hit Songs
00160195 15 songs.......................$12.99

Fingerpicking Hymns
00699688 15 hymns $12.99

Fingerpicking Irish Songs
00701965 15 songs.......................$10.99

Fingerpicking Italian Songs
00159778 15 songs.......................$12.99

Fingerpicking Jazz Favorites
00699844 15 songs.......................$12.99

Fingerpicking Jazz Standards
00699840 15 songs.......................$12.99

Fingerpicking Elton John
00237495 15 songs.......................$14.99

Fingerpicking Latin Favorites
00699842 15 songs.......................$12.99

Fingerpicking Latin Standards
00699837 15 songs.......................$17.99

Fingerpicking Andrew Lloyd Webber
00699839 14 songs.......................$16.99

Fingerpicking Love Songs
00699841 15 songs.......................$14.99

Fingerpicking Love Standards
00699836 15 songs $9.99

Fingerpicking Lullabyes
00701276 16 songs.......................$9.99

Fingerpicking Movie Music
00699919 15 songs.......................$14.99

Fingerpicking Mozart
00699794 15 pieces.....................$10.99

Fingerpicking Pop
00699615 15 songs.......................$14.99

Fingerpicking Popular Hits
00139079 14 songs.......................$12.99

Fingerpicking Praise
00699714 15 songs.......................$14.99

Fingerpicking Rock
00699716 15 songs.......................$14.99

Fingerpicking Standards
00699613 17 songs.......................$14.99

Fingerpicking Wedding
00699637 15 songs.......................$10.99

Fingerpicking Worship
00700554 15 songs.......................$14.99

Fingerpicking Neil Young – Greatest Hits
00700134 16 songs.......................$16.99

Fingerpicking Yuletide
00699654 16 songs.......................$12.99

HAL•LEONARD®

Order these and more great publications from your favorite music retailer at
halleonard.com

Prices, contents and availability subject to change without notice.

0322
279

  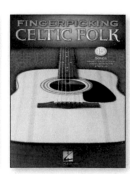  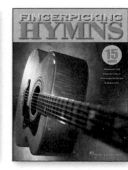